AF506087

Mama's
a Mammal

Mama's a Mammal

Quinta Cattell Kessel
Hundred Acres Farm, Storrs, Connecticut

Illustrations by Margaret May Kessel

Vernissage

VERNISSAGE PRESS, BOULDER, COLORADO

Copyright © 2004, Quinta Cattell Kessel
and Margaret May Kessel, Storrs, Connecticut,
all rights reserved. No part of the contents
of this book may be reproduced by any means
without the written permission of the publisher.

Published by
Vernissage Press, LLC
2200 Central Avenue
Boulder, Colorado 80301
www.vernissagepress.com

Susan Gail Buyske, editor and granddaughter
Designed by Rick Hibberd

ISBN 0-9725027-3-4
Library of Congress Control Number 2004117572
Printed in USA

Dedicated to Cattells, Kessels
and other mammals

Contents

Classification of All Living Things

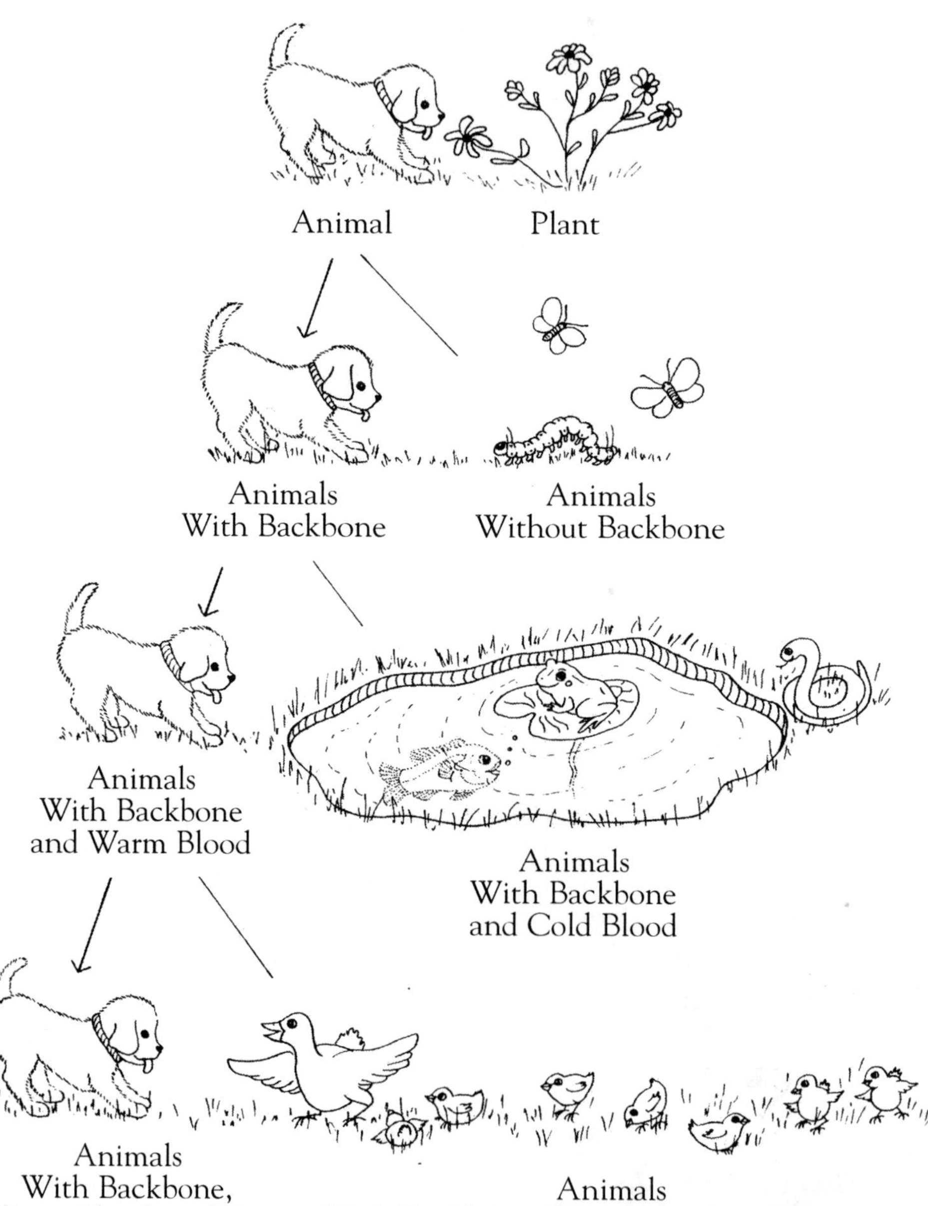

Chapter 1:
What Kind of Animals Are Mammals?

LOOK AT YOUR DOG. It is a mammal. And so are all the animals whose stories appear in this book. These stories have been written to show you the strange and interesting ways in which animals differ one from another, and also how they are sometimes unexpectedly alike; how their peculiar habits help them to survive; and how parts of their bodies have been altered to fit them for their special life situations. The animals chosen for this book are the mammals that seem to differ most from one another, in their form and way of living. Mammals are the animals that most resemble people, so we can also compare them with ourselves.

A scientist who devotes himself to the study of animals is called a zoologist. The first thing a zoologist does when he starts to study animals is to sort them into groups, as you can see in the diagram. For a zoologist, any living thing that is not an animal is a plant; and he leaves the plants for the botanist to study. The zoologist then divides the animals into two groups: those that have backbones, and those that don't, such as insects and starfish. There are a great many kinds of animals with backbones, so he divides these further into two groups: those that have warm blood, such as cats and birds and people; and those that have cold blood. The cold-blooded ones include the snakes and frogs and fish, which have the same temperature as the ground or water where they live. I am sure that any fisherman among you will have noticed that fish are cold when you pull them from the water. Naturally, therefore, the bodies of the cold-blooded animals are warmer in the summer than in the winter. (If we think carefully, we can see that there is a catch here. What about a snake in the hot sun or a lizard in the desert? These are classified as cold-blooded animals, but their blood could easily be hotter than that of a so-called warm-blooded animal. It seems to me that it would be better to think of these as animals with a variable blood temperature, and the warm-blooded ones as those with a constant blood temperature, varying only within narrow limits.)

This book is about warm-blooded animals. We need to continue our classification, however, to come to the group of animals called mammals – the only ones included in this book. Warm-blooded animals are divided by scientists into two groups also: those having feathers, which are the birds; and those having fur, which are the mammals.

And so you can begin to see why your dog is a mammal. It is an animal, not a plant. It has a backbone; it has warm blood; it has fur; and it has four legs. The most distinctive thing about all mammals, however, is that their young ones normally depend on their mothers for milk to live and grow. That means that their mothers all have to have breasts or udders of one sort or another so that they can produce milk. There is a

Latin word for breast and it is *mamma*; that is why we call this group of animals mammals. And, if the truth be told, that is one reason why we call our mothers Mama or Mommy. Only mammals produce milk, which is made in the mammary glands in the breasts or udders of mother mammals from substances furnished by the blood.

The world of animals is ever changing. We live too short a time to see the changes, but scientists have found a fascinating change in the remains of animals that were laid down with the mud and rocks millions of years ago. These bones or shells or tracks are called fossils. Many of the animals that we know now do not resemble their ancestors of a bygone day. The horse is a good example, as you will see if you look at the picture on the next page showing a present day horse and its much smaller four-toed ancestor. We find out about the ancestors of animals by digging up their bones. This work is the concern of the science of paleontology, the study of fossils.

In the far tomorrow many animals will be different from those we know today. Some will be extinct, which means that no living specimen can be found. The most successful animals are the most adaptable ones, the ones that have fitted themselves best into their environment or the situation in which they live. The successful animals have come to have effective ways of getting food, which is a first necessity; they have found ways to defend themselves from their enemies; and they have found ways to hide and shelter themselves and their young.

All animals were once land animals, and most of them have continued to live on the ground. There are some, however, that are so altered that they are now able to live entirely in the water. And there is

Today's horse is much larger than its four-toed ancestor.

one kind that actually flies in the air like a bird. These changes have come about through the survival of the animals that were the best fitted for their environments. That statement really needs a lot of explaining, and a great many books have been written on the subject. But you can easily see that the animals that could run the fastest or dig the best or find the best ways to get food were the ones that survived and lived the longest. Since they lived longer they were the ones that had more young, and their young in turn were also better fitted to survive, because parents pass their characteristics on to their children.

This passing on of characteristics is called heredity. Perhaps you have heard people say that you resemble your father or your mother, or that you have curly hair because your mother or grandmother does. Or perhaps you are unusually tall because both your father and mother are tall. These characteristics are due to heredity, and it is because of heredity that a giraffe has a long neck.

Food is necessary to life, so if giraffes could not get enough food to eat, there would not be any giraffes. Perhaps where the giraffe lived, there were a great many other animals, such as zebras and antelopes, that eat the grass on the ground; grass became scarce, so the giraffe started to reach up into the trees for leaves to eat. You can see that the tallest giraffes would get the most food and they would be the ones most likely to survive, and they would be the ones that would have the most children and the tallest children. It could be that the giraffes are still growing taller, but changes in nature are very slow and we would not be able to detect changes in the height of giraffes without exact measurements taken over many hundreds of years.

The giraffe's long neck enables it to reach food that is beyond the reach of most other animals.

I am sure you can see with your own eyes that the differences in animals are related to their different ways of living. The giraffe has long legs with which to escape its enemies and a long neck to enable it to reach a good supply of food high in the trees. The groundhog (which is also known as a woodchuck) is able to dig a safe den, and it is built squat, so it can feed in the long grass without being seen. On account of its agility, the monkey is able to seek safety in the tops of trees, while the deer depends on its speed as a runner on the ground. Often when we notice how animals live, we can see why they are the way they are.

The coloring of animals is important, too. The giraffe is dappled, which helps to conceal it while it is feeding in the sun-spotted shade under trees. The groundhog is so brown and inconspicuous that it would pass for a stone when it is still. This blending with the background is called protective coloration, and it too is the result of heredity and is a factor in the survival of the fittest. In escaping its enemies, it may be as important for an animal to hide well as it is to run fast.

As you look about you, you can see that the different kinds of animals are quite different one from another. The surprise comes when you find out how much alike all the animals with backbones are when they first start growing, before they are born or hatched. This is the embryo state of life. From the picture of different embryos (on the next page) you can see that in your early development before you were born, while you were still an embryo, you were much like a rabbit or a chicken or a fish. The miracle is that we all turn out to be so different when grown.

Comparison of Vertebrate Embryos

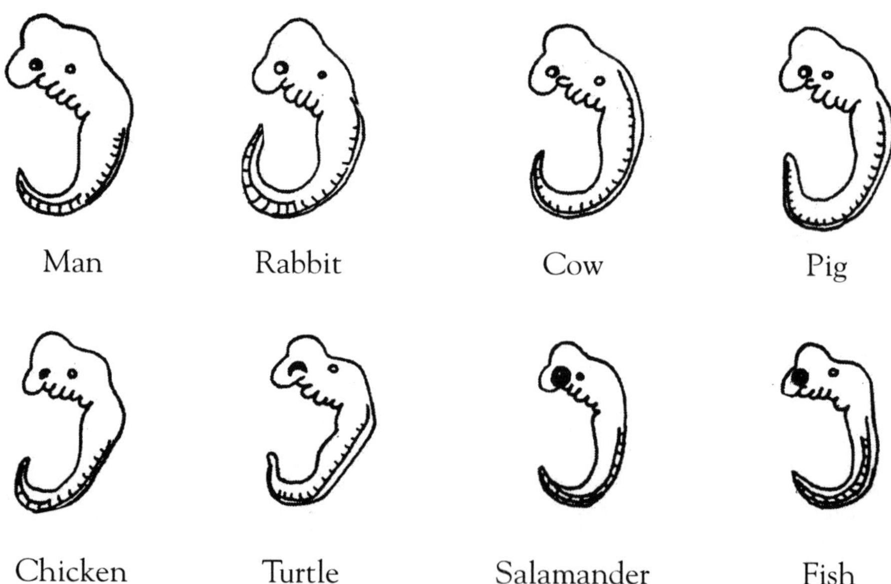

When you were an embryo, you didn't look very different from your fellow mammals, or even animals.

Chapter 2:
People

YOU WILL NOT BE SURPRISED now to find a chapter about people in a book of stories about animals. Since people are animals, it is worthwhile to think about the ways in which people are like other animals, and also how and why they are different.

People are grouped with the other animals in this book because, like them, they are mammals. They have warm blood, they have hair, which is a kind of fur, and what is most important of all, the human mother produces milk for her young, just as all mammal mothers do. People also really have four legs, but the front ones have been modified, and we call them arms. We believe that the arms were once, long ages ago, perfectly good front legs used for walking, because the bones in our arms are almost identical with the bones in the front legs of other mammals. And I will tell you a secret. People have tails. There are only about four little bones, and they are hidden under the skin, but they are just where you would expect your tail to be. This assembly of little bones is called the coccyx, pronounced as if it were "cox six." If you look at the picture of the embryos, you will see that, before you were born, you had a very fine tail. Indeed, most of the bones in your body are similar to the corresponding bones in other mammals. Even your neck has the same number and kind of bones as a giraffe's neck.

You can find a clue to the most important difference that there is between human beings and other mammals if you study the Latin words that make up your scientific name, *Homo sapiens*. If you look in the dictionary you will see that *Homo* means man, and *sapiens* is from a word meaning to have sense or to know, to be wise or discerning. And so, you can think of your self as "man knowing," understanding, thinking, planning, judging, imagining. These are words that cannot freely be used to describe any animal other than man.

The great advantage that we have over all other animals is our highly developed brain, which, I am sure you know, is housed in the head. The front part of our brain is especially large and well developed compared with that of other animals and it is this part that we use for thinking. Thinking the way we do is not evident in any other creature, and the powers of judgment and imagination appear to be ours alone. It is impossible to conceive of any animal except man that has the ability to do the reading, writing, and arithmetic that you do in school.

A great step came in our early development when man stood up on his hind legs and no longer needed his front ones to run or to support the front part of his body. When man no longer used his front feet so much for running and started to use them for other purposes, such as grasping, changes gradually came about. An important development was the position and flexibility of the thumb on the hand. You will notice, if you look at your own hand, that the thumb moves freely, much more freely than the fingers. You can use your thumb with any of the fingers to hold or manipulate delicate objects, or you can strongly grasp larger objects. This enables you to do a great many things that a dog or an elephant cannot do with its front feet because it does not have freely jointed thumbs and fingers.

The combination of an active, thinking brain and nimble fingers has led to great changes in the way that people live. When you think of the refinements of modern living it is not hard to realize how different it was to live in a cave, as millions of early people did. The cleverness of people has even affected the most fundamental of our likenesses to the other mammals, in that the human baby is no longer dependent on its own mother's milk. That is because we are so ingenious that we have been able to devise substitutes, usually made from the milk of cows. Bottles and nipples are inventions that are entirely beyond the range of ability of any other animal.

Have you ever thought about what an exciting thing it is to be able to talk? This ability we can also trace to the large and well-developed part of our brain where the center for speech is located. It may be that our ability to talk has been facilitated by the wide arch of our lower jaw, which gives plenty of room for our tongues to wag in. By talking and writing (which is a substitute for speech), and by teaching, we are able to pass on accumulated knowledge from generation to generation, and so gain more and more superiority over other animals. It is by talking and reading and teaching that our civilization has advanced and we have gained the refinements of living that we have. If we could not pass on our ideas to our children, we should be at a standstill, and perhaps have gained as little advancement as the animals we see about us.

The apes are the animals that are the most like people, and of the apes the chimpanzee seems to have the best brain. We think this because we are able to teach it more than any other animal, and except for people it has the largest brain in proportion to its size. However, there seems to be a tremendous gap between even the chimpanzee and people when it comes to planning and meeting situations. We note that, in its natural habitat, the chimpanzee has no fires, no weapons, and no tools. Only man makes and uses tools. Only man among the mammals tames other animals for his use, or tills the soil for food.

Man has been able to adapt himself to living in any part of the world, warm or cold. He has been able to devise means for staying for days under the water or up in the air. And now he is exploring the spaces far away from earth. Man has every reason to believe that he is a superi-or being. There are still many scourges of the human race that Man has not yet conquered, but it is not surprising that he thinks of himself as having dominion over every living thing that moves upon the earth, and even as having been himself created in the image of God.

Even the chimpanzee, with some close resemblances to humans, does not make fires, tame other animals for its own use, or till the soil for food.

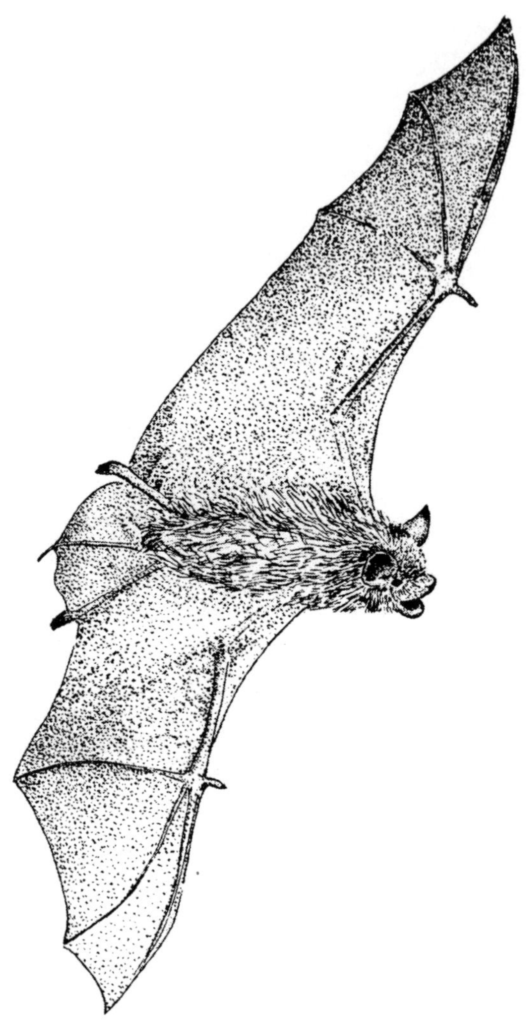

Bats are the only mammals that have real, flapping wings for flying.

Chapter 3:
The Little Brown Bat

IF YOU SHOULD GO out of the house on a warm summer evening, soon after the sun has gone down and the birds have hidden themselves away for the night, you might be lucky enough to see a little brown bat. You will not see it easily except when it is silhouetted against the pale evening sky, beating its wings with terrific rapidity and turning like a flash this way and that. By twisting and turning so adeptly as they fly, bats can catch insects in the air. We can be glad that their food consists of mosquitoes and flies and other insects that annoy us. Because they have tremendous appetites, bats may eat more than half their weight every night.

Bats are the only mammals that have real, flapping wings for flying. So-called flying squirrels are without wings and only soar or glide in the manner of a paper airplane. But bats, instead of having ordinary front legs, have limbs which have developed into beautiful wings, with webs attached to the long fingers and arms and along the sides of the body and tail. The big wings look as if they must belong to a much larger creature, but the bat has a small body about the size of a mouse, and

**Flying squirrels do not have wings
and can only soar or glide.**

like a mouse, it is covered with soft brown fur. There is no fur on the wings. Perhaps it is not strange that an animal that has become so perfectly fitted for skillful flight should be exceedingly clumsy on the ground. There is a hooked claw on the forward margin of each wing, however, which helps it when it crawls awkwardly along the ground as it sometimes does to catch insects that do not fly. When landing from a flight the bat uses the claw to hook onto a rafter or cave ceiling before it turns upside down to hang by its hind feet, its position of rest.

One wonders how it came about that bats became fliers, for we believe that their ancestors were bound to the ground like other mammals. Perhaps they first lived in trees, where they practiced leaps and flights, even as the flying squirrel does nowadays. These bats are, and presumably always were, insectivorous animals. That means that they depend on insects for food. There is a tremendous abundance of night flying insects in warm weather, and there are few creatures to compete for them, so it would seem that those bats that could reach them would have an advantage. It would seem to be a good thing to be able to fly if your food can fly. And just as with the giraffes, whose long necks are explained in the chapter on mammals, the bats that could reach the most food would be the ones that lived the longest and had the most young ones. The traits or peculiarities that were the most useful in helping them to survive would have been inherited by the young, and gradually better and better wings developed. You must not think that this happened overnight; it took millions of years.

The little brown bats can see little or nothing with their tiny eyes, which seem to be useful only to tell light from dark. But their eyes are good enough to tell them when it is evening and time to hunt for night-flying insects. They catch quantities of insects in a scoop formed by webs between the tail and hind legs, dexterously removing and eating them while in flight. Larger prey may be taken to a tree to be taken apart and eaten.

When these bats fly through the air, they have their mouths wide open. One would think that they do this to enable them to catch insects, but the tail scoop is more useful for this purpose. There is a more important, more exciting reason for the open mouth: constantly, while flying, bats make a squeaky noise so high pitched that we cannot even hear it. And all the time, the bat listens with its large sensitive ears, to hear if an echo of its squeak comes back from any object that it is approaching. In this way, the bat pursues an insect at high speed through the darkness, guided by the echo which comes back from it. And, similarly, through its echo, the bat is able, in its speedy flight, to avoid dashing itself against a building or tree or other object. To prove that the bats depend upon their ears and not on their eyes to perceive objects, a scientist plugged the ears of some bats and then they bumped all over the place. The bats would also be confused if their mouths were covered, because then they would not be able to emit the noises necessary for their built-in radar system. People use this principle of echo sounding in their radar instruments to keep airplanes from meeting in the air and to keep ships apart on a foggy night.

When the bats have had all the insects they need to eat, and morning comes, they find a place to sleep during the day-time. It may be a shed or a barn or a hollow tree, and there they hang themselves upside

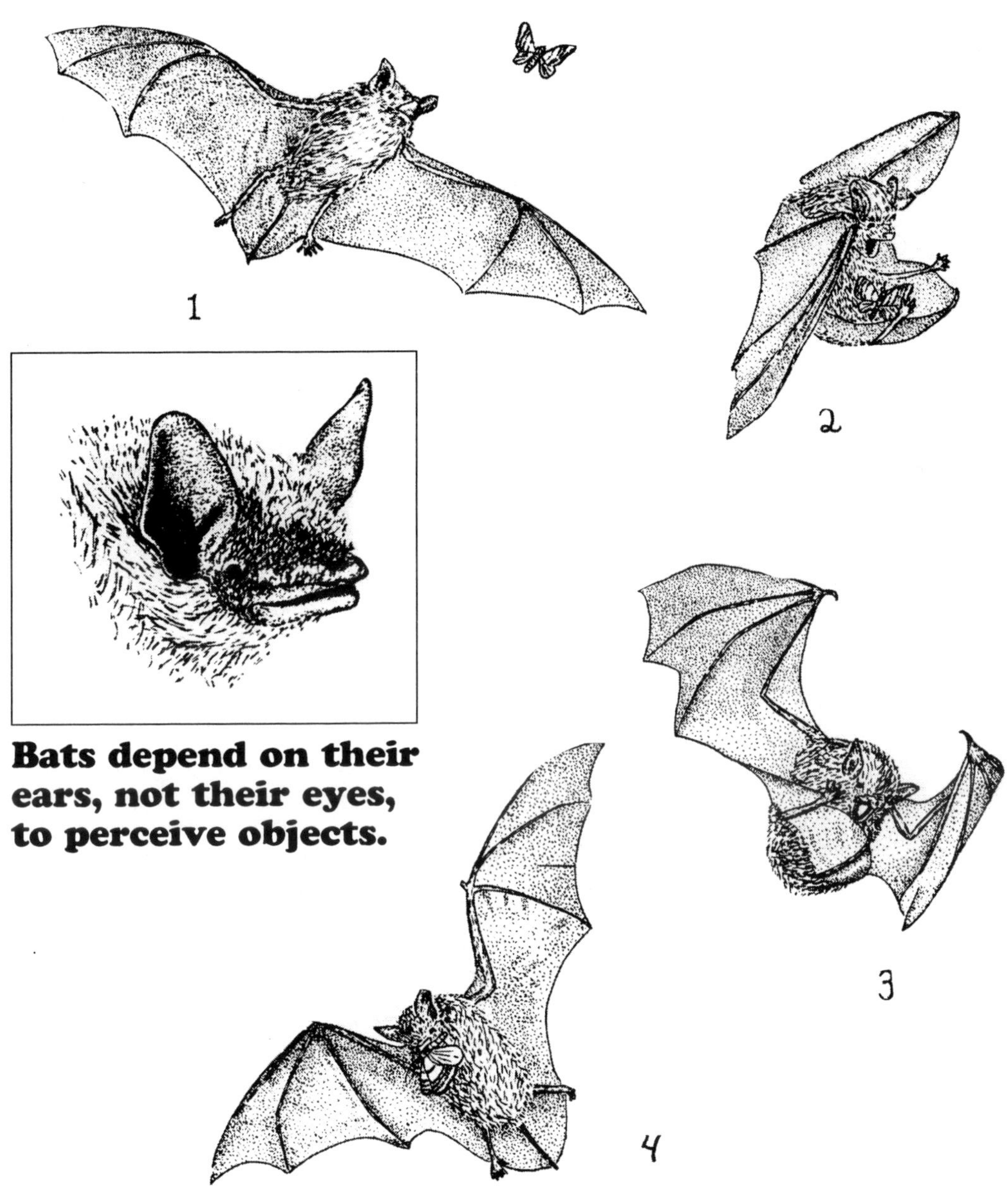

Bats depend on their ears, not their eyes, to perceive objects.

(1) The bat chases an insect, (2) catches it in its scoop, and then (3 and 4) eats the insect during flight .

Bats like to sleep in close proximity to each other. Imagine sleeping so soundly upside-down!

down by their hind feet. They fold their wings, and rest and sleep.

In the fall when the weather gets cold and insects do not fly, the little brown bats find a deep cave where the temperature will not get cold enough to freeze. There they go into hibernation for the long winter. They hang themselves up and become numb and more sleepy. To make it unnecessary to have food for a long time they hardly move, their body temperature is greatly reduced, and they breathe only about once in five minutes.

When the weather gets warm in the spring, the bats come out of hibernation, and in May or June the young are born. Usually there is only one young bat for each mother and she takes wonderful care of it. When the baby is about to be born, the mother hangs herself up by her hind feet. There she spreads her scoop like an upside down umbrella, forming a safety net, and catches the baby when it is born. The tiny baby has no fur, and for some days its eyes are closed. It clings to its mother's breast, where it can get milk when it is hungry. It is generally believed that the mother carries the baby bat with her in the evening when she flies out to catch insects for herself. After a short time the young one will become too heavy for her to carry, and she will park it in a safe roosting place. There it can hang by its own hind feet while she is gone. Before many days have passed, the baby bat will be taking practice flights, and it soon will join the other bats on fine evenings in their tireless roller coaster pursuit of insects. The young bats will spend the rest of the summer growing, and after their long winter sleep, they will start to have young ones of their own. And so the cycle will be complete and a new generation will begin.

In the world of Nature a creature that has few natural enemies usually has few young ones. Because the little brown bat has only one baby, we can assume that it has to meet comparatively few hazards. There is only one night-flier that would like to have a bat for dinner and that is the owl. The owl's manner of flight however, is much too slow to make it dangerous to a bat. Probably the most important hazard is bad weather, which may interfere with finding food. But one baby a year seems to be enough to ensure that there will always be little brown bats. When you come to the chapter on the rabbit you will see that its story is quite different.

It is not surprising that many people think that bats are birds, but you know that the mother gives the young milk, so you know absolutely that the bat is a mammal. And it has fur, not the feathers of a bird. Of course, the confusing thing is the wings, but by studying the bones in the wings, scientists have found that they are basically the same as the bones in the front legs of a dog or any other mammal. It is just that the bones in a bat's wing (or front foot) have developed into long thin bones that have membranes attached, so the bats are able to fly like a bird.

Bats have been a symbol of evil for centuries and many people are afraid of them even now. There are a number of superstitions about them. One is that if a bat gets caught in your hair you will have an unlucky love affair within a year. Do you think anything could be more ridiculous? Why would a bat get tangled in your hair when it has an excellent radar system and extraordinarily quick flight to prevent such accidents? Most superstitions are rather silly and are due to ignorance. If you reason them out carefully, you can see that they cannot be true. Almost everyone knows the superstition about groundhogs. No doubt you have heard that they come out to see their shadows on the second of February, and if they do, are scared back into their holes for six more weeks. Many people believe that because of this there will be six more weeks of winter. I wonder if you believe this story too?

The white tail of the cottontail rabbit can serve as a safety device. When a chased rabbit turns suddenly and hides its tail, its pursuer loses sight of it and rushes past.

Chapter 4:
The Cottontail Rabbit

PERHAPS you have never stopped long enough to wonder why the underside of the tail of a cottontail rabbit is pure white, just like a piece of cotton. One reason is that at times it serves as a safety device. Cottontail rabbits are beset with a great many enemies, including dogs and cats and foxes that chase them. When they are chased, they scamper, with their little white tails bobbing behind them. Suddenly they turn and the white underside of the tail no longer shows. The pursuer, who has had his eye fixed on the little bit of white fluff, rushes past, confused and not knowing where the rabbit has gone.

Another trick that rabbits have to protect themselves is to "freeze" or squat down motionless on the ground, where their grizzled brown fur makes them inconspicuous. They do not stir unless an enemy comes too close. Their tremendous ears and twitchy noses are an adaptation that senses the nearness of danger and helps them to survive in their dangerous environment. So too are their great leaping hind legs.

It seems that almost everything a cottontail rabbit does is done to try to keep itself from being the dinner of some other animal. Life is risky even for young cottontails, and they must be constantly on the watch for danger, even when they scamper about in play. The young ones play tag with fits and starts and sudden freezing. In this way they train themselves for the day when they must elude the hungry pursuers.

In the course of a New England summer, a mother rabbit may have three or four nests full of young rabbits. Since there are five or six young in each, you would think that you would see rabbits everywhere. However, I can think of no creature that meets so many dangers in its daily life. People with guns are probably the worst hazards. But it is hazardous, too, for the rabbits to cross over the highways at night, because they become blinded and confused by the lights of the cars. They are also beset by owls or hawks or snakes, by dogs or cats or weasels.

It is little wonder that the rabbit has so many more young than the little brown bat. If there are not enough enemies to control the number of rabbits or if an area becomes too crowded, starvation and disease will take a heavy toll. Perhaps only one out of twenty young rabbits will survive to start a new family the next summer. And this is the reason that we are not overrun by rabbits. If all the rabbits that are born lived to old age, we should have a hard time to grow food for ourselves or for our domestic animals. They would eat all the grass in the pastures and the grain in the fields.

Despite their many enemies, rabbits do have fun; when courting in the springtime, a pair of grown rabbits often have hopping play. One rabbit leaps straight up in the air and the other dashes underneath. Then they turn about and the other one jumps. It makes a pleasant picture to think of them as they gambol thus in the moonlight, although you are unlikely to see them because if you are nearby they will be quietly hiding in the shadows.

Because of their many enemies, rabbits choose their nesting sites where the young will be as safe as possible. Most of them make their nests in open fields near the fence rows or hedges. The nest is strategically placed so the mother has a clear view of the approaches on three sides while she herself is on the fourth. Here she is near thickets or brush piles where she can hide, and at the same time she can stay nearby and feed while watching the nest and hearing if the young ones squeak. If the young are disturbed by an intruder, the mother rabbit will attack the enemy viciously and try to drive it away. She knows how to use the claws of her hind feet to punish an intruder.

In preparing the nest, the mother digs a shallow, oval depression, only about four or five inches deep. To make it comfortable and warm, she lines it with soft bits of grass and with fur which she pulls from her own body with her teeth. About five or six young ones make up the family of rabbits. After they are born, the mother covers them with a felt quilt made from grass and more fur from her body. At first the young, like the new-born bats, have no fur and their eyes are tightly closed. The openings of their ears are sealed too, and the ears themselves are little bits of shrivelled things lying on their heads. The mother never feeds them in the daytime, because she does not want any movement near the nest to attract the attention of a cat or other enemy. She comes in the darkness, probably several times in a night, and carefully pulls back the cover she made to keep the young ones warm, and then she nurses them as all mammal mothers do. When they are satisfied, she pulls the cover

over them again and scatters a few leaves and grasses over the nest so it is completely concealed. The father rabbit takes no interest whatever in the young rabbit family. Indeed, if he appeared, the mother would attack him with great vigor and chase him right out of her territory.

Until they can see and hear, the baby rabbits are quiet and sleep most of the time, but changes come quickly. By the time they are seven or eight days old, their fur is well grown and their ears stand up properly as a rabbit's ears should. Then they can hear with their ears, and their eyes are open too. In about twelve days they come out of the nest for the first time, but they stay close by, each one near its own little hiding place in the grass or hedgerow. They start to nibble tender green sprouts and at night they snuggle back in the nest to keep warm. In two more days, more or less, they leave the nest forever and start to lead independent lives. If people matured as rapidly as rabbits do, I think you would change from a baby to a grown person in about a year. Compared with a person a rabbit spends a much smaller part of its life in growing up.

Chapter 5:
The Beaver

BEAVERS ARE LAND ANIMALS, but they are so much at home in the water that we call them amphibious, which is a word meaning having two characteristics. During the long ages when beavers were becoming better and better adapted to living in the water, slow changes came in various parts of their bodies, which made them different from other mammals. Their lungs, their noses, lips, and teeth, their hind feet and tail, and their fur have become specialized and have helped them to lead safe and warm lives in and near the water.

Ordinarily a beaver or a pair of beavers does not live alone. When winter comes, the three or four young ones that were born in the spring are still living with their mother and father. The young ones that were born the year before are also still in the family group, and they all live together and work hard together to build a safe and satisfactory beaver community. With the old ones, and the young ones, and the old young ones, there may be eight or ten beavers all together in a colony. When the next batch of babies comes the following spring, the oldest young ones have to go out in the world and seek their fortunes, starting new communities in other ponds and streams.

Sometimes when a person has been working extremely hard for a long time a friend may call him an "eager beaver." The beaver certainly is a hard worker and, except for man, it is the greatest builder in the world of mammals. Since much of its work is done below the surface of the water, the beaver has special features that enable it to work efficiently while submerged. It has large oversized lungs, which make it possible for it to stay under the water for as long as ten or fifteen minutes. This ability also helps the beaver to hide from its enemies, because in that time it can swim far away without being seen. You can experiment to see, but I do not think that you can hold your breath for much more than one minute. To save itself from having to consciously hold its breath when it dives, the beaver has valves in its nose that are closed automatically when pressed by the water.

A beaver does many underwater chores, which involve working with sticks. It seems as if it would be awkward for a beaver to carry and work with sticks and other materials held by its teeth while under the water. This feat is possible because the beaver has flexible and stretchy lips and cheeks that close behind its great gnawing teeth when subjected to the pressure of the water. This enables it to hold or gnaw the sticks or carry chips in its mouth without getting water in its throat. There is also a space in the beaver's skull between the front teeth and the grinding molars at the back — as there is with all rodents. Rats, mice and squirrels are also rodents, and the scientists consider them all fairly closely related because of the similarity of their teeth. The beaver is the largest rodent in our country.

The beaver's hind feet are large and have webs between the toes almost like the feet of a duck. And, like a duck, it is an excellent swimmer. It has a broad, paddle-like tail that is used as a rudder to help steer the beaver as it swims. While in the water the beaver has another use for its tail. If it senses danger when it is swimming, it brings its tail down sharply on the surface of the water and this sends it into a sudden dive. The sudden dive makes for safety, and the slapping of the tail causes a sharp noise that warns any other beaver within hearing to beware of danger. You could make a similar sound by slapping the surface of the water with the flat side of a board or canoe paddle.

For its warmth in the water, the beaver has a short, thick, silky coat of under fur, which holds a layer of air next to the body so the skin will not be in contact with the chilly water. This soft coat is protected by long, coarse, oily guard hairs that help to keep the water out. When a beaver comes out of the water it wipes and combs itself dry with its webbed hind feet.

The beaver has an effective built-in woodworking tool in its front teeth, which are long and strong and sharp. It needs no ax or saw. Moreover, the backs of these gnawing teeth are made of a softer material, which wears away more quickly than the front, so that as the teeth are used for constant cutting of wood, they stay as sharp as chisels. Like your fingernails, the teeth keep growing so they do not wear completely away. But on the other hand, the beaver must keep gnawing or its ever-growing teeth will prop its mouth open.

Their strong, sharp teeth enable the beavers to be their own lumberjacks as well as builders. With their teeth they cut down trees, sometimes quite large ones, and then they cut them up into logs from two to eight feet long. When a beaver cuts down a tree, it stands on its hind legs, propping itself with its broad tail. Then it cuts out a notch as high as it can conveniently reach, and a second notch three or four inches below the first. With a twist and a yank it tears out big chips between the notches. When the tree starts to fall, the beaver scampers away so it won't get hurt.

Life in the water has led the beavers to accomplish truly amazing feats of engineering. Of these, the dams that they build in streams are the most important type of construction because all their activities depend on them. Their purpose in building dams is to hold back the water in a stream so that it will form a pond deep enough for them to build a special kind of house and to store their winter food supply. They like to be able to go in and out of their houses without being seen by their enemies, so the only entrance to their houses is below the surface of the water. For this reason, the ponds must have water deep enough for the beavers to get in and out, even if the ice in the wintertime is a foot thick.

The dams are built of sticks and logs, reinforced with brushwood, and packed with dead leaves and mud and stones. Vegetation growing on the top sends down roots that bind and strengthen the structure. And from year to year the dam is constantly repaired and increased in thickness by the beavers. They are aided in that work by the debris that washes down the stream and lodges against the dam. A dam may be ten feet through at the base and hundreds of feet long.

A beaver house is an impressive accomplishment as well. The beavers live on the floor of the house, which is in the air a little above the level of the water. It is here that the young are born and nursed by the mother. Logs as long as six feet are used to roof it over. Then the beavers plaster it all over with mud and leaves and stones, which they push into the cracks with their noses and paws. To bring this mortar, they grab double armfuls, and by using their broad, flat tails to steady themselves they can walk upright even to the top of their house. Cracks in the roof let in plenty of fresh air. When the house freezes solid in the wintertime, the beavers inside are safe. If the house should be disturbed, they plunge downward through their underwater doorway and swim far away under the water before coming to the surface to survey the danger. They often have a burrow ready in the shore of the pond, at the end of which is a room above the level of the water, where they can go to wait out danger if necessary.

When a beaver family has cut down all the trees near the pond where it lives, the beavers must go farther away for timber. It may be too far for them to drag the heavy logs, so they dig canals, sometimes hundreds of feet long. Then they float the logs on the water in the canals, and thus the hauling becomes much easier. When a beaver swims with a log, it holds the log with its teeth and uses its tail as a rudder so it will not swim around in circles. Beavers often smooth off a track down the slope of a hill, which makes it easier for them to drag the logs to the water.

Beavers do not hibernate or sleep through the long winter months, so they must have food available when the ice is thick and the snow is deep. In the autumn the whole colony gets together and gathers a great supply of sticks with the bark on. These are stored in the bottom of the pond, where any beaver can easily swim to them from the underwater door-ways. To keep the branches and sticks from floating, the beavers weight them down with stones and mud. When the beavers are hungry, they take sticks up into the house and eat the bark. To get rid of the peeled sticks after they have eaten the bark, they add them to their dams and houses, which get bigger and bigger every year, and no doubt better and stronger. If the colony has established itself in a favorable site it may go on for many years, with some members leaving and new ones being born. One beaver house that I saw near Fairbanks, Alaska, has been occupied for at least twenty-five years and has grown to be 51 feet long and 39 feet wide. It stands more than seven feet above the level of the water. Unfortunately beavers sometimes make a nuisance of themselves by stopping up culverts or flooding land that we want to use for our own purposes.

When the settlers first came to America the beavers were plentiful, but they were trapped ruthlessly for their fur. Their fur helped to make the country rich, but naturally the beavers became scarce. Today there are laws to keep the hunters from trapping too many beavers and our conservation officers often catch beavers to take them to new localities so that more and more colonies will be started. In Idaho they have transported beavers in airplanes to suitable sites, and then parachuted them to the ground in specially built boxes, which break open when they hit the ground. The beavers spill out unharmed and soon start to work on new engineering projects. With measures such as these being taken by our conservation officers we can be sure that there will be more and more beavers in the future.

Chapter 6:
The Opossum

NOT MANY PEOPLE KNOW that the opossums that live in the United States are close relatives of the kangaroos that live in Australia. One of the reasons they are grouped together by the scientists is that the mothers of both of these animals carry their young ones in a warm, fur lined pouch in front of them. This pouch is a sort of traveling nest where the young can easily get milk from their mothers while they are tiny and where they are protected from the cold and from their enemies. Scientists call these animals marsupials, a word meaning pouch or pocket.

Even where opossums are common, you would not often see one, because they sleep all day and roam in the woods at night to look for food. They look much like big, overgrown rats, almost as big as a cat or woodchuck. They live in woods and swamps and spend much of their time in trees. They climb well, because their hind feet have thumbs much like the ones you have, and so can grasp firmly just as your hands do. They also have something you do not have and that is a long, grasping tail, which they can wrap around a branch for safety or use to hang themselves up in a tree. They can use the tail, too, to gather and carry bunches of dry leaves for their nests. A good way to describe the tail is to call it a prehensile tail, which means that it is adapted for grasping.

No doubt you have heard the story about how this animal "plays possum" when it is frightened, pretending to be dead until the danger is past. It becomes limp and falls down on its side, it shuts its eyes, and its tongue hangs out of its mouth. If you were to pick it up, it would not have any more stiffness then a rag doll. But if you should go away, it would soon be over. This action makes it seem as if the opossum is a clever animal but there is another explanation. It isn't pretending; it just can't help itself. When danger comes it is so frightened it can't run; it gets paralyzed with fear and falls in a faint. It suffers, really, a kind of shock. Perhaps lying so still helps it to escape its enemies, and thus it could be that its weakness is an aid to its survival.

Baby opossums are born only thirteen days after they have started to grow within their mother, so when they arrive they are tiny and undeveloped. They are so small that a dozen of them could be held in a teaspoon. Kittens and puppies are much larger and look much more like their mothers when they are born. That is because they grow as embryos within their mother for 63 days before they are born, and have had time to become much better developed. A dog mother weighs only about 25 times more than a puppy, but an opossum mother weighs about 8000 times more than one of its babies. If a puppy grew as much as a baby opossum does in growing up, it would be as big as an elephant.

In spite of the fact that baby opossums are born tiny and weak, and blind, there is one remarkable thing that they do immediately, and their lives depend on it. While a newborn opossum seems to be little more than an embryo, its front legs and feet are strong and well developed. With the aid of these, it manages to crawl through what must be a forest of fur for such a little creature, until it reaches the opening of the mother's pouch and then gets inside where it will be warm and safe. There, in the fur-lined pouch, it is just about as warm and well protected as when it was an embryo before it was born. This protection may be necessary because the young are born so soon and undeveloped.

Inside the mother's pouch there are 13 nipples to which 13 babies can attach themselves and have a drink of milk at any moment. Their mouths almost grow to the teats, so tightly are they fastened by the suction of the baby's tongue, and they do not let go for weeks. The young grow amazingly fast, and after the first week they are almost ten times as big as when they were born. In about eight or nine weeks the mother's pouch begins to get crowded. The babies then crawl out and onto her back, where they cling tightly to her fur as she goes about her business of finding food. No doubt they take turns going back into the pouch for more milk until they are weaned. Gradually they learn to find and eat the same food as their mother. She eats almost everything, whether it is plant food, like berries and fruit, or animal food, like frogs and snakes or insects. Animals that have the habit of eating all kinds of food are called omnivorous. When one stops to think about it, one realizes that people are also omnivorous.

Camels have adapted themselves to living in temperatures as high as 140 degrees Fahrenheit.

Chapter 7:
The Camel

CAMELS ARE INTERESTING CREATURES and different from other mammals, because there are many ways in which they have adapted themselves to living in a terribly hot, dry climate. Parts of the Sahara desert where they live have temperatures that often go as high as 140 degrees Fahrenheit and there may be great stretches of sandy wasteland between available supplies of water.

Everyone has heard that camels can go for a long time, even a week without water, although the weather may be extremely hot. As a matter of fact, if there is enough grass and other vegetation for them to eat, camels do not need water at all, and do not drink even if they have a chance. There is some water in the vegetation, which will suffice because the camel uses water most economically in its body. It does not need to drink as much as most animals.

In olden days people thought that camels stored water in their humps, but this could not be true because their humps are solid fat. The fat provides the camels with a reserve of energy when food cannot be found, in which case the hump gradually shrinks. Like cows, camels have more than one stomach, and until recently people thought that when camels drank an enormous amount of water at one time they stored it in one of the stomachs. Lately scientists have found out that this is not true either. Camels have no special reservoir for water. When they drink a great deal at one time, as they sometimes do, it is to replace the loss of water in the tissues, and not to store it for future needs. The mystery of the camel's ability to go for a long time without water is solved when we understand that it conserves every drop of water it drinks.

A camel does this in several ways. It perspires so little that its skin always feels completely dry, and you can imagine what a difference that makes in the amount of water it needs. If you get hot, you perspire and your skin becomes damp or even wet; a great deal of water is evaporated. The drying of the moisture cools your skin and helps to keep your temperature normal. A dog does not perspire, because it has no sweat glands, but when a dog pants it is achieving the same cooling effect by the evaporation of moisture from its tongue and throat and lungs. If your temperature goes up even one or two degrees above 98.6 Fahrenheit, which is normal for you, you feel ill. But a camel is different. It still feels all right if its temperature goes up as much as eleven degrees – from 93 degrees, which is its usual temperature, to 104 degrees. It seldom needs perspiration for cooling itself.

A camel conserves a great deal of water by eliminating little in its bodily functions. Its dung or manure is practically dry and it passes only a small amount of water in the form of urine from its kidneys even when it has all the water it wants to drink. Of course, a camel cannot go without water forever, but it does have a life-saving provision if conditions are extreme; so far as I know, it is the only animal that does not lose water from its bloodstream during prolonged thirst, drawing instead from the muscles and other tissues. Loss of water from the blood would cause thickening that would endanger life.

In northern lands most of the animals wear a thick coat of fur to protect them from the cold. This keeps the warmth of the body from escaping. The camel has thick fur too, but that is to protect its body from the heat of the desert. In either case, you see, the fur acts as a layer of insulation to retard changes in temperature. Arabs and other people who live in the hot Sahara wear long, heavy woolen clothing for this reason.

With its ability to travel long distances with little water, the camel is a boon to the people that live in the desert. The camel with one hump, the dromedary, is used mostly for riding or for light loads. It has longer legs and is much faster than the camel with two humps. The camel with two humps is more heavily built, with shorter, thicker legs, and it carries a much heavier burden. It can travel only about 25 miles in a day, while the riding camel may go 50 to 75 miles. Camels have softly padded feet that spread out and keep them on top of the sand. Their eyes have long, thick lashes for protection from the windblown sand. Even these small adaptations for getting along in its special way of life in the hot and sandy desert add something to the ease and comfort of the camel's hard life.

The camel has been domesticated for thousands of years, and it is seldom found now in the wild state. The desert people use its fur for clothing and its skin for leather. They use its meat and milk for food, much as we use our cattle. Indeed, the scientist notices that our cattle and the camel are fairly closely related, because among other things, they are both ruminants and therefore have several stomachs and chew their cud.

Whales live in the water as fish do, but they are warm-blooded mammals that breathe air and nurse their young.

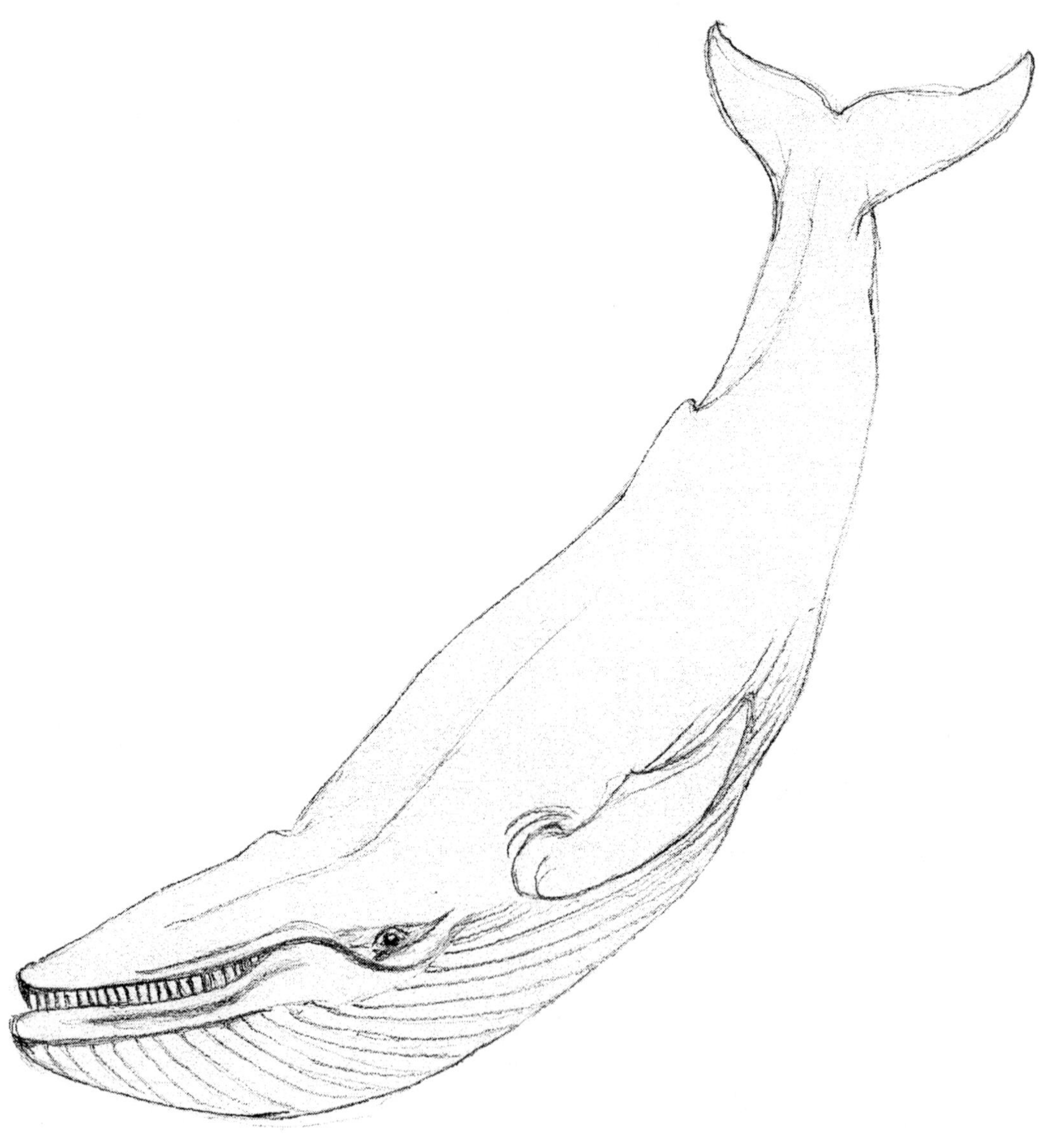

Chapter 8:
The Great Blue Whale

IF YOU HAVE EVER THOUGHT about whales you probably thought they were fish. That is not surprising, because they live in the ocean and never come out on dry land. But unlike fish, they are warm-blooded mammals that breathe air and nurse their young. And though today they must always live in the water, whales would drown just as surely as any land animal if they could not come up for air. If we stop to compare a whale with a fish, we notice that a fish lives below the surface of the water all the time, but a whale cannot. In order to live, all creatures must have oxygen in their blood. Whales and land animals obtain it by breathing air, which contains oxygen. In their lungs, the oxygen passes through the thin cell walls into the blood stream. Fish, on the other hand, get their oxygen from the water as they take it in their mouths and let it pass over their gills on its way out. The blood in the gills receives the oxygen from the water also through thin cell walls, which shows you that the gills of a fish are the equivalent of the lungs of a mammal.

It is interesting to observe also the difference in the tails of whales and fish because each is the way it is for special reasons. The tail of the fish is vertical, or straight up and down, and when it is waved from side to side it propels the fish through the water. The tail of a whale is horizontal, or flat, and when it is pressed downward, the whale's head naturally bobs upward, so it can come up quickly for air when it needs it. This up and down motion of the tail flukes also makes the whale a powerful swimmer.

We believe that once upon a time in the long ago the ancestors of whales lived on the land, and there is even evidence that they had legs. Perhaps on the land they had too many enemies, or more likely, there was not enough food for them. Perhaps they found more food by wading into the water and thus gradually went deeper and learned to swim. There is much that we do not know, but we can see many indications of changes that presumably took place as the whale gradually became fitted for life in the sea. One interesting adaptation of the whale for life in the sea concerns its tears. It is quite obvious that a whale does not need watery tears to keep its eyes moist as we do, but it has greasy tears, which protect its eyes from the irritation of the constant immersion in salt water.

If whales once lived on the dry land, what do you suppose happened to their legs? It is easy to imagine, and it seems to be true, that the front ones were modified and became the paddle-like flippers that the whale now uses for steering and for balancing its body in the water. Inside the flippers are the same bones that are found in the front legs and feet of animals or in the arms and hands of people, although some of them are fused together. As for the hind legs, there just aren't any. They are not needed, because the great tail flukes have taken over the function of propelling the whale through the water. That whales once had hind legs is shown by the fact that there are still two small leg bones buried deep in each side of the body just where you would expect them to be if there were legs. This may remind you that you have little tailbones under your skin that are of no use to you.

During the time (millions of years) when the whale was becoming adapted to life in the sea, differences came in its respiratory, or breathing, system. By experiment you can notice that you can breathe through either your nose or your mouth, as the whale no doubt could do when it was a land mammal. Now, however, it can breathe only through its nose, which is on the top of its head. If you get food or water mixed up with air in your throat you are likely to choke, but a whale would not have that trouble because it has a separate tube for the air to pass from the nose to the lungs. When you swallow you have to close off your air tube with a valve so you will not choke.

The top of the whale's head is a handy place for the nose, or blow-holes as the nostrils are called, because it enables the whale to breathe without exposing itself unduly above the surface of the water. The location of the nose on top of the head is just another of the adaptations that the whale has to make life in the water safer and more comfortable.

When whales spout, they spout from their blowholes or nose. Before they dive they take a vast amount of air into their lungs, and then when they dive, valves in the holes are closed automatically by the pressure of the water. The whales may be under the water for some time, maybe ten or even twenty minutes. During this time, the air in their lungs becomes warm and moisture laden. When they come back to the surface, they expel this steamy air with great force from their blowholes and it condenses as mist in the cool air. That is what makes the spout. It used to be thought that the whales took water in their mouths and spouted it out through their blowholes, but we have seen that that is impossible because there is no connection between the mouth and nose. It is unfortunate for whales that they spout, because it is a signal that tells whale hunters where to find their prey.

One might think that if a whale were stranded on the shore, as occasionally happens, it could survive because it breathes air. But, unhappily, when there is no water to support its body, the whale's great weight causes the lungs to be compressed and it cannot breathe. The whale no longer has strong rigid bones, because it does not need them for life in the water, and if it is accidentally on land, the ribs collapse. The water supports practically all the weight of the whale, or of you, if you are in the water. If you were to put a weighing machine in the bottom of a swimming pool and try to stand on it while submerged, you would find that you weigh not even as much as one pound.

Under the whale's skin is a thick blanket of fat, or blubber. I can think of several ways in which this adaptation might be helpful to the whale in the special life it leads in the ocean. Fat is not as heavy as water, and so, you know, it floats, and thus it helps the whale stay easily near the surface of the water where it spends most of its time. This great layer of fat may serve, also, as a food reservoir at times when food is scarce. Its very presence suggests that there are seasons, or times in its travel to far places, when food is not plentiful. The layer of blubber is excellent insulating material too and it probably serves to protect the warm body of the whale from the cold water of the Antarctic ice pack where it spends at least part of the year. When first born, the whale calf does not have a layer of fat, but I am sure that is because it is born in warmer waters.

The whale baby is the biggest animal baby there is – almost as big as a full-grown elephant. Fortunately it can swim as soon as it is born. Remembering that whales are mammals, we know that the mothers must give their young ones milk when they are first born. Nursing is a problem because the baby cannot suck very long at a time under the water without coming up for air. The problem is solved by the mother, who always has a quantity of milk ready when the baby is hungry. She has muscles that she can contract suddenly so that she can quickly pump a lot of milk all at once into the baby's mouth. She may also roll on her side to make it easier for the young one to reach a nipple. The milk is extraordinarily rich and nourishing. The cow's milk that we drink is about four percent fat, but a whale's milk is about 38 percent fat, which must account for the fact that a baby whale gains about 200 pounds a day.

The blue whale is the biggest animal that ever lived. To tell you that a grown one may be over a hundred feet long and weigh over a hundred tons doesn't really give you a good idea of its immensity. To help visualize its size and shape, you might compare it with a jet airliner that will carry a hundred or more people and, in your imagination, replace the wings with a pair of flippers and take off the upright part of the tail. Then you would have a pretty good mental picture of a blue whale. Both the jet and the whale are streamlined – the plane to reduce the resistance of the air at high speeds and the whale to make fast swimming easier. The whale has a smooth skin and no external parts such as an ear or a nose or even hind legs to break the smoothness of the surface of its body as it slips through the water. You could hardly say that you can tell that a whale is a mammal by its fur, because it doesn't have any. It really should, but all it has left is a few bristles near the mouth. In becoming adapted to constant submersion in the water where fur could be of no use, the whale has lost any fur that it might have had when it was a land animal.

It is a good guess that the sea is exceedingly rich in the food whales like to eat or they never would have grown to be so large. And I think it is another good guess that they are larger now than when they lived on dry land. I think this because it is impossible to conceive of an animal so large able to move with enough alacrity on the land to reach the tons of food it needs every day. In the water the whale is a graceful creature, and it swims thousands of miles every year. In the summer the blue whale is found most commonly in the cold waters around the Antarctic ice pack where its food is abundant. It leaves this region in the autumn and migrates to warmer waters where the calves are born. Scientists do not know the migration routes of whales nor where they stay with the calves before they are weaned.

The food of the blue whale and how it gets it makes a strange story. In the first place, even though the blue whale is about as big as a house and has a huge mouth, it has a tiny throat, which is so small that a grapefruit would probably get stuck in it. Therefore, it must get its food in small packages. In the second place, it doesn't have any teeth. Instead the whale has a great strainer, called the baleen, which hangs from the roof of its mouth. This baleen is composed of many long, thin strips of a horny substance, called whalebone, which has a fringe of bristles along the edges.

The chief food of the blue whale is shrimp that are like small, soft crayfish, about one or two inches long. In some places in the ocean, where there is plenty of food for shrimp, there are an enormous number of shrimp for the whale to eat. The whale hunts for these areas and then swims rapidly through them with its monstrous mouth open. It closes its mouth on a great quantity of water crowded with shrimp. The whale doesn't want to swallow all that water, so it strains the water out through the bristles of the baleen and then swallows the shrimp which slide easily down the whale's little throat. The food of the whale is called krill, which I am sure is a brand new word for you.

Scientists have recently discovered that whales make underwater noises and they think they find their food by echo-sounding. That is, they swim along making noises and if they approach an area in the sea that is crowded with krill the sound bounces back, enabling the whale to locate its dinner. The story of the bats in this book tells how they too find food and avoid objects by sound echoing back to them.

It seems ridiculous to compare a whale with a bat or dog, but they are placed in the same animal group because, as you have seen, they have certain basic similarities that all mammals have. Particularly, they are warm-blooded and they nurse their young. Whales have traces of fur, and they have four legs, even though the front legs have by now been modified into flippers and the hind ones have almost disappeared.

There are thousands of kinds of mammals of diverse sizes and shapes, but if you keep these points in mind, I think you will always be able to tell whether or not an animal is a mammal.

The hippopotamus spends most of its time in shallow rivers, with most of its three to four tons of weight submerged under water.

Chapter 9:
The Hippopotamus

IN GREEK, hippopotamus means river horse, even though the hippopotamus is certainly not a relative of the horse and bears no outward resemblance to it. It does live in rivers, which is the excuse for its name. Surprisingly, however, the hippopotamus is a relative of the common barnyard pig. It is so broad that it makes double trails in the jungle. One side of the trail is worn by the feet on the right side of its body, and the other is worn by the feet on the left side, like the tracks left by cars in a grassy lane. Like its name the hippopotamus is long and cumbersome; it is only about four and a half feet high, with stumpy legs, and yet it may be as much as fourteen feet long. Its shape seems as absurd in a flat sort of way as the shape of a giraffe in a tall sort of way. But we have seen that when an animal has a prominent characteristic it usually helps it to fit in a special kind of environment.

Like the beaver, the hippopotamus leads a double life, partly in the water and partly on the land. Its special environment or habitat is in and near shallow rivers, where the water is only a bit deeper than the hippopotamus is tall. Its plan of life when in the rivers is to be lazy and inactive, and not to swim a great deal, so there is no need for the hippopotamus to be an accomplished swimmer. Most of the time it spends sleeping in the shallows. The hippopotamus has a way of submerging so that only its nostrils, which are on the top of its snout, and its eyes, which are in a high, bony ridge of the skull, and its small ears show above the surface of the water. Then you would little suspect that three or four tons of hippopotamus are attached underneath the water.

If the hippopotamus does want to travel far in the water, instead of swimming, it prefers to let some of the air out of its lungs so it will sink; then it can run along the bottom of the river, and cover many miles with a minimum of effort. One day I was lucky to see some underwater movies of hippopotamuses that were taken on the bottom of a river. It was fascinating to see that these monsters, when buoyed by the water, move with the lightness and grace of ballet dancers. They have to come up for air only once in four or five minutes. Ordinarily we expect an aquatic animal to be streamlined to make it a good swimmer, but anyone can see that the hippopotamus has made no progress in streamlining its body. It is safe to assume, therefore, that swimming does not play a vital part in its life, and that it does not need to swim to get its food or escape from its enemies. Why, then, do you suppose that a land animal like the hippopotamus spends its days wallowing in the mud or resting in the water? My guess is that it does so for reasons of comfort, to escape the daytime heat and pestiferous insects of the tropical climate. Also, since it is such a heavy animal, it must be a relief for it when the water supports most of its weight, as it does with that other huge animal, the whale.

Besides being amphibious, by living on land and in the water, the hippopotamus is herbivorous. Herbivorous is a word used to describe animals that eat only plant food. I suppose you could call them vegetarian, as you do a person that does not eat any meat. The hippopotamus eats the reeds and grasses in and along the banks of the rivers. Because it needs a prodigious amount of food to support its huge body, it may range several miles from the river's bank in search of it. It has a tremendously big mouth, which suggests to me that in that hot, damp climate, the vegetation grows lush and thick, and can be gobbled in big bites. To travel on land for food it must have good walking legs, and that could be the reason that this aquatic animal, even though it spends at least half its life in the water, has not developed flippers or webbed feet or any other aid to swimming. If the hippopotamus did have flippers like the seals or the whales, it would not have legs, because it is the legs of the seals and whales that have changed into flippers to make them better swimmers.

The very fact that the hippopotamus feeds on the plants in the rivers makes it useful to the people that live in the region. It keeps the rivers from becoming choked with vegetation, so they remain open for navigation by small boats. The cleared rivers also provide a much better environment for fish, and more fish feed more people.

The skin of the hippopotamus is about two inches thick, but it is said to be quite tender, perhaps because of the alternate drying in the hot tropical night and the prolonged soaking in the water in the daytime. There are glands in its skin that secrete a thick, sticky, pinkish stuff, which we think provides a protective covering and guards the skin from drying. This covering might also prevent undue softening of the skin from soaking all day in the warm water of a tropical river. When early travelers saw the strange pinkish secretion they reported that the hippopotamus "sweats blood."

The mother hippopotamus has only one young one at a time, an indication that this animal has few natural enemies. The baby stands when it nurses, and for some reason it prefers to stand in the water. The water must not be too deep, because the baby has to be able to hold its mouth high enough out of the water to reach its mother's udder.

No doubt the most dangerous enemy for the hippopotamus is man. Sometimes, too, it is attacked by lions when it roams on land in search of food. If it should be attacked by lions, it rushes to the water, which probably discourages the lions. The rivers where the hippopotamus lives are infested with crocodiles, but it seems to live peacefully with them. The presence of the crocodiles may account, however, for the fact that the baby hippopotamus spends much of its time riding on its mother's back or remaining close by her side when she is in the river.

Some day the hippopotamus may become extinct. That is, we shall no longer be able to find living examples of it. It lives now only in Africa, chiefly in Ethiopia, and its numbers are decreasing. We know that it once lived in England, because its fossil bones have been found in the valley of the Thames River, which runs through London. If you look in London for it now, I am sure you will find it only in the zoo. Why do you suppose it no longer lives along the rivers in England?

My guess is that it must have been an easy target for spears and traps, and so was exterminated by man. The hippopotamus is such a strange and wonderful animal that we hope there are wise men who will keep other men from destroying it entirely, and help to keep it living on this earth a long time. Some countries have built wild-game preserves of some of the areas where the hippopotamus lives. These preserves enable us to enjoy watching these creatures at work and at play, while leaving them in peace.

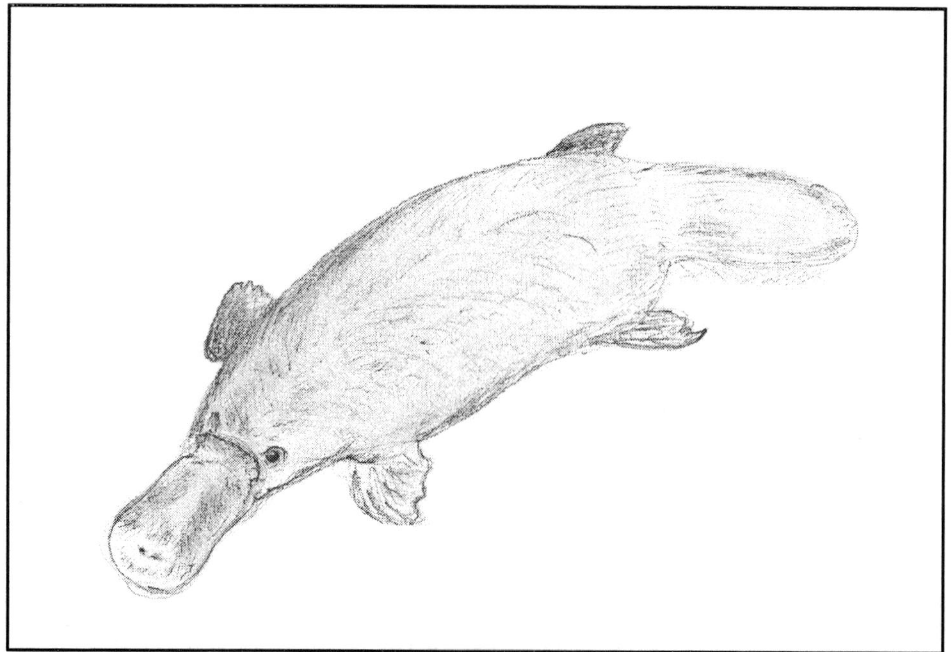

The duckbill platypus is like a living fossil, because it has traits that have disappeared in other mammals millions of years ago.

Chapter 10:
The Duckbill Platypus

THE DUCKBILL PLATYPUS is the animal that time forgot. Although it sounds like a contradiction, we can think of it as a living fossil. Scientists would naturally have expected that it would have disappeared millions of years ago, but it still lives in Australia and Tasmania. The duckbill platypus is considered primitive, because in some ways it has not developed into a complete mammal. The bones of its skeleton are more like the bones of the reptiles, such as the turtles and snakes and dinosaurs, than they are like those of modern mammals. Scientists believe that the mammals developed from the reptiles many millions of years ago, so we can imagine that there may once have been mammals that were even more like the reptiles than the platypus. This animal with its mixture of reptile and mammal features helps to support the scientists in their theory. The fact that the mother platypus produces milk for her young shows without any doubt, however, that it is truly a mammal. It also has soft, brown fur and warm blood, which as you know, are mammal characteristics.

The platypus is unusual as a mammal in still other ways. It has a bill somewhat resembling the bill of a duck, and it also has webbed feet. This does not mean that it is any way related to the duck, but that it lives in the same watery environment and therefore has use for the same kind of natural tools, much as the beaver does. The bill of the platypus is soft and rubbery and very sensitive, and it is used to nuzzle in the mud for grubs and worms. With its webbed feet, the platypus is an expert swimmer, so it is able to add to its diet with shrimps and tadpoles and other small water animals.

The platypus lives in quiet, cool streams and it digs its burrow in a bank with the opening usually just above the surface of the water. At the end of the burrow, as much as sixty feet from the opening, the platy-pus has a large nest of reeds and roots. When the mother feels that it is time for her young to be born she retires to her burrow, placing several large plugs of earth in the channel after her so that she will not be dis-turbed. When the two or three eggs come they are cemented together, perhaps so they cannot roll away and be lost in the nest, but more likely to make them easier for the mother to hold while she incubates them. She has to keep them warm for some days before they will hatch, and this she does by clutching them to her body with the hairless underside of her tail and rolling herself into a ball.

At first the young are naked, blind, and helpless. They are dependent on their mother for bodily warmth. It is easy to imagine that she holds them in the same way she held her eggs. One of the reasons scientists think of the platypus as a primitive mammal is because it has no udder or teats of any kind with which to suckle its young. In spite of this shortage it is a true mammal, because the mother does produce milk. The milk oozes from almost invisible pores on her underside, and the young suck and lick it from her fur.

Did you notice the most surprising thing about the platypus? The female lays eggs instead of giving birth to live young as we expect mammal mothers to do. We expect the birds and most of the reptiles like snakes and turtles to lay eggs, but not mammals. Of course, you know that all mammals have eggs, but they do not lay them. Instead the eggs grow as embryos within the mother until they are ready to be born as babies. The platypus has to take care of its eggs after they are laid and keep them warm, just as a bird must incubate its eggs before they will hatch. The embryo grows inside the eggshell until it is fully developed, and it is time for it to hatch. The plan of creation is not so different; it is the method. With both, a young animal is produced and that is the important thing.

Conclusion:
Following the Trail

I HAVE ENJOYED WRITING these sketches because I am eager to show you that true things about animals are just as remarkable as anything we can imagine in a make-believe story. Peter Rabbit and other animals that talk like people are fine for storytime reading, but I have been thinking that many of you may be famous scientists some day and that you will be interested in reading about real animals, and in thinking the way scientists think.

Of course, you will realize that I have not been able to find out by myself all of the things that I have written about animals. Although I have raised and observed and studied animals directly, I have also read many books by important teachers. I have tried to find the newest ideas and facts for you. The trouble is that even these teachers say opposite things, and then I don't know what to tell you!

I was reading about camels in a three-volume set of books, where the author said that if their drivers or others abused them they would spit at their tormentors. What an interesting observation for me to write into my sketch about camels! But I wanted to make sure that he was right, so I wrote a letter to a man who had just come back from a year in the Sahara desert studying camels for the United Nations. He said the camel does not spit, but he explained that the camel's cousin in South America, the llama, does. He well knew because he had once received in his face a liberal amount of whatever it does spit!

Now I wonder! I could think of a possible explanation of why an observer might think he saw a camel deliberately spit, but my explanation would not be a scientific fact. Camels are ruminants like cows. Which means that they eat their food twice. First they eat a lot of food in a hurry, and then later they bring it back up into their mouths to chew it at leisure while they are resting. This is called "chewing the cud," and it is easy to see that a cough or a sneeze at the moment that there is rumen or cud in the mouth would make a mess, and someone might think that the camel had spit.

If you go to Egypt where camels live, or South America where llamas live, I hope you will look into the matter for me. You would have to ask questions of many people, but most important, you would have to see the act yourself a number of times and find out what makes the camel or the llama do it. It is hard to believe that they are able to think well enough to direct an attack at a particular person because they are mad at him. I believe most scientists would say that this is an automatic reaction to fright or discomfort, and they would call it the "defense mechanism." Perhaps you have held a grasshopper in your fingers and have noticed that brown juice oozed out of its mouth, or you may have caught a garter snake that made such a horrible smell that you did not hold it long. You can see how these acts, performed automatically without thought, defend these animals from their enemies and allow them to escape. It could be that the camel spits for a similar reason.

I also found contrary statements about the little brown bat. You would be more likely to be able to help me with this problem because this bat can be found almost anywhere in North America. I read three books in which the authors said that the mother carries her baby with her when she flies out in the evening to catch insects to eat. Then I read another in which the author said that there is no evidence that she does this.

If you can find where a colony roosts, I wish you would go there in the early morning and in the evening when the bats come in and go out. Bats usually sleep in colonies or groups during the day, in old attics or barns or caves. You would have to sit quietly and watch closely to see if the mothers were carrying the babies; and after they had gone out, you would want to search the rafters or cave ceiling carefully to see if any very young ones had been left. You would want to try to find out how old the babies are when the mother does leave them. Since there is no nest, it seems reasonable to suppose that she might carry them while they are naked and might get cold, and then leave them when they have grown some fur.

But just thinking will not make it so, and you should never have your mind made up when you make scientific observations. Just study carefully and see what is there, always keeping a written record of what you see. This is the scientific method, and this is the way to gather facts to add to what we already know, and so to increase our knowledge of the world about us.

In science it is a good idea to be a little skeptical and not believe too readily statements that are not based on certain knowledge. A case in point is the so-called "combing claw" on the fourth toe of the hind feet of beavers. The writers say that the beaver uses this to comb the water from its fur when it comes out on land. I find it difficult to believe that the peculiar claw on the fourth toe is specially formed for this purpose. It is very small to be used to comb such a large animal, and it seems more likely to me that the beaver might wipe itself off with the edge of the webs between the toes of the hind feet. It would be difficult to observe how the beaver uses this queerly shaped claw, but I think someone should do some research on this question and I don't see why it should not be you.

These contradictions have made me realize that even a naturalist who had spent all his life studying animals could not possibly have had a chance to see with his own eyes all the activities of all the creatures that are described in his books. The authors must take some of the information from others on faith just as I do. The books in which I have felt the most confidence are those written by authors who have spent many years or most of their lives studying just one kind of animal. Surely they must be in the best position to know what they are writing about.

You should not make the mistake of thinking that the brief histories in this little book tell the whole story of these animals. I have tried to tell you only some of the more amazing things about them. Much more is known, and still more is not known. Even the big books I have read are not complete, and the stories of the commonest animals that live in the fields and woods near us have not yet been completely told. There is more to be found out about groundhogs and squirrels and frogs and snakes; there is still a wonderful chance for you and other young naturalists to discover their secrets.

Quinta Cattell Kessel

MRS. QUINTA CATTELL KESSEL was born on August 11, 1900 and grew up in Garrison, New York. Her father, James McKeen Cattell, was the editor and publisher of several scientific journals, including *Science*. The fifth of seven children raised in what was then a relatively isolated location, Mrs. Kessel and her siblings were educated by tutors. As a result, Mrs. Kessel entered Cornell University as a special student and was the first person to be awarded a master's degree from Cornell without having a bachelor's degree, which she could not obtain without having a high school diploma. Mrs. Kessel studied zoology and entomology at Cornell, where she also met her future husband, Marcel Kessel. They raised five children on a farm in Storrs, Connecticut, where Mrs. Kessel put her zoology training to practical use. Mrs. Kessel's life-long interest in the natural world and her pleasure in sharing that interest are expressed in *Mama's a Mammal*. This book was written during the 1950s. Mrs. Kessel passed away in 1967.